WHAT A LOAD of SCRAPS!

More possibilities for taming your unruly scraps

by Penni Domikis

www.cabininthewoodsquilters.com

CONTENTS

©2014 Penni Domikis for Cabin In The Woods Quilters

Developmental Editor: Penni Domikis
Cover and Book Designs, Illustrations
and Photography: Cabin Digital
Piecing and Quilting: Penni Domikis
Editor: Some Farsighted Guy
Published by Cabin Digital
Fredericksburg, VA

Attention Teachers:
To obtain copies of this text for
teaching, you may contact Cabin
In The Woods Quilters through the
website at:
www.cabininthewoodsquilters.com
or by emailing us at:
cabininthewoodsquilters@gmail.com

What A Load of Scraps!: More
possibilities for taming your unruly
collection of scraps.
1st Edition: May 2014
ISBN: 978-0-9835325-4-5(spiral pbk.)
Printed in the United States of America

ACKNOWLEDGEMENTS:
Thank you to ...
Some of the wonderful unknown
partners in the world who let me
bounce ideas off of them and love
every one. My husband who makes
our house a home, helps me live in
peace and harmony in the woods,
helps me keep the peace and
harmony at bay when it threatens
to encroach on our flower beds and
brings me a much needed cup of
coffee or glass of sangria whenever
the need arises. Much love to you all.

Introduction

In 2011, while buried in my sewing studio under a mound of useless leftovers, an idea was born... and that idea culminated in the release of my first book, ***All Scrapped Out!*** This was a guide for your journey into scrap quilting that defied all rules. A real solution to a growing problem, the "save your scraps" dilemma.

The following year I released another book, ***Still All Scrapped Out!*** with more of the same. Using some additional rulers I found lying around as templates, I created another book of ideas for tackling that giant pile of castaways.

With the release of my second book came a wave of clients. Shops and guilds from all around called to have me visit with them and explain how you could make a real honest to goodness masterpiece without pre-cutting or pre-pressing all those scrap pieces. So I began a tour of sorts - a "Cabin Fever Tour" we called it - to visit with as many guilds as I could to share this unbelievable method.

It's not so hard to believe really. Quilters have been making quilts this way for a long time. We all know that is precisely the way quilting got started. Women getting together, using leftover clothing or feedsacks and such to make blankets to warm their loved ones. Some were better at making patterns than others but the method was all the same. But somehow the "use what you have" part of the equation was lost. Perhaps the women wanted to make a particular pattern and could not get the desired look from leftover pieces. Perhaps they wanted their quilt to match a particular decor. I am not certain where or when but somehow women migrated into fabric stores and quilt shops to purchase a pattern and the accompanying fabrics for a project and never looked back.

Now you will not hear me say that you should stay away from quilt shops. Not at all. I highly encourage you to shop at those local places, visit with the staff, purchase the patterns and the fabrics (because I would never deny you new fabric) and become a part of the quilting community. Making a perfect masterpiece from a great new line of fabric is always appealing and I have a closet full of UFO's (Unfinished Objects) to prove that theory.

What I suggest is that you take a look back when those perfect projects are completed and make another masterpiece from all the parts left over. That second masterpiece will have less rules and less points. It might have more than one particular line of fabric or have many different colors. It might have crooked pieces and all the seams might not match. Despite all these unusual qualities it might wind up being your most memorable project. It might be filled with colors you didn't know you liked. It might be born of conversation instead of instruction. It might just surprise you. I believe that is the reason these books have been so popular. I have taught many quilters to let go of the rules... if just for a moment. I have taught these quilters not to overthink a color or a seam. I have taught them to have a conversation with each other while they sew and to share fabrics and ideas. It really is a very fun project.

Over the three years since these books have been released I developed my own line of templates. Not rulers because they have no lines and no measurements. They are just shapes of acrylic that you can use to make your masterpiece a reality. My goal for the templates, as with the books, was to make them reasonably priced and only there for your convenience. Afterall, who needs another ruler.

In this new book, **What a Load of Scraps!**, I have continued this tradition making another guidebook with new designs just in case you need a little help. I have incorporated some more modern fabrics to keep with the changing times but as always your quilt will resemble you. I have tried a new modern shape, the "tumbler", which is one of my favorites and offers lots of possibilties (some of which will be saved for the next book). Check out the **Tumber Fun** quilt, the **Evenflow Rainbow** charm tumbler quilt, and the **Tumbler Runner**, the small project in the book. Making a table runner from the Tumbler Template is something new and unique.

Crazy Signature Scraps is a signature project for sharing with your quilting buddies. A memory quilt made completely from scraps starting with crazy quilt blocks made from leftovers. **Easy Diamond Delight** uses a 60° triangle to make a wonderful diamond quilt with traditional scrap quilt tones. **Hidden Hexies** is another 60° triangle quilt with a few hidden surprises. **Diamond Play** uses a 90° triangle (half-square triangle blocks) to make an interesting all over quilt. It's really fun to turn the blocks and see what you can some up with. The only question is where to begin. **ZigZag Pizzazz** uses the half-square triangle and some modern fabrics to create a fresh simple look for any scrap project. Made completely with leftover pieces that were not in strip form, this scrap quilt takes our method to a new level.

Far and away the best quilt in the book is **Crazy About Pinwheels**. Don't get me wrong... I like everything in the book and they are all my favorites. There is just something about making a "free" quilt completely from leftovers. What do I mean? Well... our pinwheel quilt is created from all of the leftover borders, strips sets and scrap ends from one of our other quilts. It's the most amazing thing. After trimming all of my borders and completing a top, I realized all of the fabrics left over and decided to use up every last piece in another quilt top. I cut the leftover strip sets into blocks, the border pieces into blocks and all of the scraps went together to make a couple of crazy quilt blocks. Up on the design wall it went and another quilt was born. I consider it a "bonus" quilt and I think when you see it you will be in love with it too.

I hope that after reading this book you truly embrace your scraps. Don't try to change them into something they're not. Accept them for who they are and open your imagination to the possibilities that they offer. Challenge yourself to look at all those leftovers and castoffs in a new light and make a masterpiece of your own.

~Happy Quilting

Penni

Loving and Embracing Your Scraps

Now that you have selected this book, you should make a commitment to yourself to make something from YOUR scrap stash. So the first thing to do is get to know what you have. I was shocked when I first started thumbing through my collection. There were fabrics in there that I didn't even recognize. Then I remembered that when I was going through my "applique phase" I bought scraps from other people. I bought bags of scraps from quilt shops and quilt show booths and picked up random pieces that other people wanted to throw away. So there were lots of fabrics in those baskets that I had never used before. That was a good thing because I had many colors and patterns to choose from.

When you are selecting a project to make with your scraps you don't want to pick something that uses 5-inch squares and then find that your baskets are filled with two inch strips. I know when I began saving I chose pieces that were probably way too small to make something if I was being realistic about it. When I was organizing everything I did thin things out a bit and throw away part of my scrap stash. Most of what I threw away were corners that I cut off or little bits too small to hold. You really should go through what you have and make a decision if keeping all of it is right for you. Deciding what pieces are most useful may help you decide what to keep in the future and help keep your scraps at manageable levels.

To begin organizing, I filled a basket with only scrap strips. I wasn't selective about the size of the strips or the color of the strips. I just decided that anything that was between 1-inch and 6-inches wide and more than 6-inches long was a "strip" (basically, a rectangle). Once I organized all the "strips" into one basket then I started coming up with ideas to use them. You may want to keep pieces that are more square in a basket with charm squares if you like using those. I put anything that resembled small squares or triangles (and in some cases leftover pieces of blocks) into another basket to be used for something else. For this book, I also used scraps from my "leftover hunks" category. Those are pieces leftover from a bag or small project that are too small to be a fat eighth and oddly shaped but no less adored. I used these to cut out solid pieces from my smaller templates. You may occasionally notice that some of my "shapes" are a solid piece of fabric. I probably had a large enough hunk that no strip piecing was necessary.

If you are into Reproduction fabrics and you would like to make a scrap quilt made entirely of those then you will need to pull those pieces out of your general scraps. I found when organizing my scraps that because my reproduction quilts were often made from FQs, those scraps were much larger pieces and were better suited to store away to cut something out of later (such as parts for a sampler). The majority of those fabrics did not make it into these quilts although occasionally you might find a smalll piece or two embedded in my quilts.

I usually try to create at least one completely random scrap quilt in each book but in this book I created all the quilts from leftovers of the other two books. For previous quilts I would create a perfectly chosen strip set from a particular color tone and may have only needed one or two triangles cut from the set. I saved the strip sets and reused them (Hidden Hexies, Easy Diamond Delight, and Diamond Play) in this book. I also used quite a few pieces large enough to cut an entire template.

You may notice in some quilts (ZigZag Pizzazz and Evenflow Rainbow) that some of the blocks are pieces and some are solid. The solid blocks are cut from larger scraps that were able to accomodate a whole template. Many times I use fabrics that other designers sell off after they make a project. I may like the looks of their fabric lines but don't need large pieces to make my quilts. Never turn down someone willing to give your their "destash".

Some quilts are made from the scraps from a particular line of fabrics (Tumbler Fun and Tumbler Runner). Often times when I am making my quilts and notice there are quite a few scraps left over I may plan a scrap project immediately and make use of those scraps that are already coordinating with each other. They may all be from the same line or they could be from many coordinating fabrics and colors (Crazy About Pinwheels) that I put together myself.

I tried to put something for everyone in this book. It is meant to be the inspiration for your masterpiece so I really hope you will take my suggestions and run with them. Most of the quilts in this books are lap quilt size. You will make your quilt whatever size you want to suit your needs and your scrap stash. Don't be afraid to mix things up or branch out on your own. There is always at least one student in the class that reaches for the stars on the first try.

Resizing Your Projects

I realize that the quilts shown in this book may be smaller than the normal desired size for your project. You may need to adjust the size of the patterns to something more suiltable to you. If you want a larger quilt you will make more blocks from your scraps. I have not provided the fabric requirements in the book for the amount of scraps you will need for your quilts because they should be made from your scrap stash. Instead I have indicated how many blocks you need to make to complete the quilt as pictured. It takes very few scraps of each color to make these blocks.

If you have never worked with triangles before you may find a few of the measurements below helpful when planning your project. Here are a few of the measurements of the block sizes in the quilts that can be used to approximate the number of blocks you may need for the size project you intend to make.

Hexagons* - If you cut 6-inch 60° triangles your completed hexagon blocks will measure approximately 10-inches x 12-inches.

Diamonds* - If you cut 6-inch 60° triangles to make your diamonds your blocks will be about 5½-inches x 10½-inches.

*These measurements are for general thought process only. You should use them only to begin planning your quilt and resizing to fit a particular project. All measurements in your quilt should be based on the ruler you choose and your personal seam allowances. I am just giving you a guideline to get you started.

Selecting the Perfect Fabrics for Your Project

I know that some of you will take one look at a random fabric scrap quilt, cringe at the different fabrics within and say to yourself, "I would never make something like that." That's OK. These are your quilts and you have to make what appeals to you. However, some of us are looking for a great way to use up our stash and make something out of all the little memories of projects long forgotten. I know for me... I found strips in my stash from my first big quilt that I ever made, which I neglected to quilt properly and which will probably not make it to the next decade. So now that I know better, it's great to have a piece of my quilting history preserved in something else that might last a little longer.

Before you go about selecting your fabrics, figure out what project appeals to you the most. I tried to organize the projects by difficulty. Some of you have amazing skills with color. So you are looking at some of the more planned projects and getting some wonderful ideas. Some of us have better skills at reducing or expanding a pattern to suit our needs. The great thing about this book is that it's really designed as a jumping off point for you and your creativity. I would love to see you expand on the ideas and make it even better. You should not feel confined by this book.

If you are choosing a color organized project, you have the option of beginning by sewing your divided color strips together and figuring out a border afterwards or starting with a border fabric and choosing the tones within that border. As a rule with any scrap quilt, deep reds, browns, greens, blues and grays tend to be great neutral colors and allow the fabrics in the center of the quilt do the talking. In previous books I have also used black to offset some of the colors. Many of the modern quilters are using grays and beiges as there neutrals.

If you choose to start with a colorful border fabric, lay all possible strips across the border fabrics and pull out any fabrics that were standing on their own. You may not want anything to "pop out" at you. Perhaps you want all the fabrics to blend. If you look closely in my quilts you will notice that they are not necessarily all the same tones, but they do blend nicely.

Grouping Your Assets

I find this style of quilting makes the perfect quilting bee project. If you have a group that you love to sew with, this is a really wonderful project to get your sewing group to do together. Pool your resources together to share scraps, tools and ideas. Like many of you, I have a wonderful group of women that I like to sew with. Every group has many personalities within. There are always one or two in the group that hoard fabrics and probably have the best scraps and always one or two that buy anything and everything they can get their hands on and might have one or more of those rulers I will talk about in the next few pages. Every group always has at least one person that is fabulous with color. She is the one that has the stash to die for and always has that little piece of something that you need to complete your project. This would be the perfect time to get your sewing group together and pool your resources.

Sometimes when working on a particular project you need to concentrate really hard to keep from making a mistake and sewing something in the wrong direction. I know that I spend hours in my sewing room wishing I had my friends around me to talk to but the minute I get together with them at a retreat I get nothing done. There seems to be a breakdown between the nerve that runs my mouth and the nerve that runs the foot pedal on the sewing machine. However, the good thing about these projects is that getting started takes little concentration. You can get all the strips you need sewn to make a project in about an hour or two, and you can share all your tools and scraps and have great fun while doing it. I love teaching this technique as a workshop because the students always seem to have so much fun. Make sure you consider getting together at your friend's house or a local church or quilt shop and try this out for a day of fun with your quilting friends.

This program is also a fantastic way for shops to get in touch with their customers and their quilting community. If you are a shop owner concerned about promoting this book because it will discourage customers from purchasing fabric, I assure you that is not the case. Borders, backings and bindings will still be needed for these designs. Also, nothing makes a quilter want to purchase new fabrics than using up some of their stash on a project. My favorite thing to do after I finish writing a book is to replenish all the stash fabrics I used in the borders of my scrap quilts. Of course, that takes me right to the local quilt shop where I get to experience everything new in the world and I always see something that I can't live without.

Using the Tools You Already Own

One of the recurring themes of this book is "using what you have." So I wanted to create designs using the tools I had lying around as well. I don't know about you, but I am fascinated with gadgets. It doesn't matter whether they are electronic or just a handy piece of plastic. I am easy prey for any quilting tool or specialty ruler on the market, as long as it makes my life easier ... and maybe makes me look like I know what I'm doing. On occasion, I purchase a ruler or tool and use it once for one quilt and it winds up in the ruler drawer. This book encourages you to get those rulers out and use them. Even if it's not listed in this book, try it out and see what you can make of it.

I used four different types of rulers/templates during the making of this book: a standard square ruler (9½-inches or larger), a Omnigrid Right Triangle (90° angle x 45° triangle), a Clearview™ 60° Triangle Ruler, and a Tumbler Template. Over the years that I have taught this method some of the ruler manufacturers changed the names of their rulers or, in some cases, stopped manufacturing the rulers all together. Last year in order to accomodate our customers needs we began manufacturing my own acrylic templates at the cabin so that you were never without what you needed if you couldn't find it elsewhere. As always I encourage you to use what you have first. I have listed our CWQ product number next to each ruler/shape that you may not have. If you need one, call us or order online on our website.

- <u>Standard Square</u> - I chose to work with an Omnigrid® 9½-inch square ruler. I have standard squares in various sizes. This size was perfect for these projects. It was slightly larger than all my blocks but not so large as to be cumbersome. You could get away with using any square larger than this but try not to pick one so large that it's hard to maneuver on your cutting table.
- <u>Omnigrid® Right Triangle (90°/45°) Ruler (CWQ-90T6 or CWQ-90T8 Triangle Templates)</u> I was told in a beginning quilting class that I really needed this ruler. It was one of the basic necessities of quilting. I have to admit that I have only used it once before the making of my scrap quilting books, not because it isn't useful, but mostly because the person who convinced me that I needed it so badly was not in my studio to show me how to use it once I brought it home. I found this ruler quite handy once I made the correlation between the size of the triangles it measured and the size of a finished square. If you have arranged quilts on point and have needed to cut setting triangles, I find that cutting them with a triangle ruler really is much easier once you get the hang of it. You can cut smaller strips that meet your needs and "flip flop" the ruler quickly.
- <u>Clearview™ 60°Triangle Ruler 1-8-inches (CWQ-60T6 or CWQ-60T8 Triangle Templates)</u> I bought this ruler as a specialty item to make some quilts for myself. I love making quilts with the 60° triangle because they are so easy to line up and the piecing goes together in simple rows. It can be used for kaleidoscope quilts as well. I chose to cut my blocks from the 6-inch measurement. Most of my strip sets measured just slightly larger than this ruler with approximately 3 strips per set.
- <u>Trace and Create Tumbler by Clover (CWQ-TRAP6, CWQ-TRAP3 and CWQ-TRAPCH Tumbler Templates)</u> - I have never used this Clover tumbler. I have simply made my own but this particular template comes in multiple sizes and may be available at your local quilt shop. It seems to be reasonably priced and provide lots of options when quilting. Any tumbler will do. If you have made or found your own design... go for it.

Once you make a few projects from this book (and I hope you will because they are simple, quick and easy projects to make), take a glance around your sewing room/studio and look for rulers or tools that you already own that might make an interesting look when used with your strips. The best part about "playing around" with your scraps is that if you make something you don't like, you can feel comfortable throwing it out or tossing it aside without regret. Remember that whatever you make please make sure that you cut all your blocks from the same template/ruler so they all fit nicely together.

I recently taught some advanced quilters at a Modern Quilt Guild this technique and they decided to cut and make multi-sized blocks. I cautioned against doing that because I wanted their project to be uncomplicated and fun. They did it anyway and I am sure that eventually they completed their project and it looked spectacular but it is definitely not recommended.

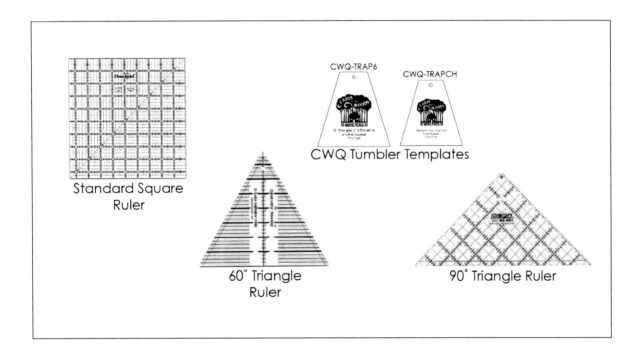

Stitching Your Scraps and Making Your Blocks

Since you have read this far into the book, I suppose it's time to begin explaining how to tame these unruly scraps into something really beautiful. Be prepared. Some of you may cringe at a few things I am about to say. I understand. I have been through the same classes and have been taught the same "rules" that you have about piecing. One of the most important rules that I learned was "accuracy." If you are not accurate in your cutting and your piecing then your quilt won't turn out right. It will pucker, it won't fit together, or you will cut off valuable points and viewers will wonder about your skills.

We will bend that "accuracy" rule in this book. It's not because I don't like rules or am determined to defy authority, it's simply because those pieces that you have been saving have not been following the rules. No one told them to stay in that basket and keep their edges intact. No one told them not to fray or to get mixed up with the other sizes. So it is impossible to follow the rule of accuracy. We will eventually follow all the rules, but not during the initial piecing.

How you piece your strips together will ultimately be dictated by what quilt you have chosen to make. The quilt pattern will determine how wide or long your strip sets need to be, but we will all begin the same way. Pick up those leftover pieces and lay them out together by length. You will have some strips that will be really short (6 - 12 inches long). Some of your strips will be of medium length (18 - 24-inches). Some of the strips will be the entire width of your fabric (WOF) which will be 39-44-inches in length. See ... not even the fabric companies follow a complete standard all the time.

To make things easier on yourself, you will stitch the short pieces together into strips sets as shown. They will not all be the same length so you will do your best to make them work together. Of course, the medium pieces will all be stitched together and the long pieces together to create long strip sets. When these strip sets are cut into block sizes, they will become the same size and you will be able to stitch them together.

strip set stitched together

Be sure to read the instructions at the beginning of each pattern. Each block requires a certain width of strip set to cut the blocks. It doesn't take as many pieces sewn together to make a block as it may sometimes appear. You might be surprised how quickly your pieces are completed. I know that I was. I was also surprised at the number of quilts I was able to make from my scrap baskets without even making a dent. Keep that in mind the next time someone desperately wants a charity project. You have plenty of fabrics for creating quick and easy projects just lying around in those baskets waiting to be tamed. Also remember that in some cases you will be able to use your template directly with your larger scraps without strip piecing at all. Don't forget about those larger pieces too, especially if you are using a small size template/ruler.

Dealing With Uneven Pieces and Wonky Troublemakers

I came up with this idea from looking at antique quilts. Have you ever really looked at antiques? We see them in magazines, museums and quilt shows. Some of us purchase them for hundreds or thousands of dollars. We use them as ideas for creating our designs and even imitate and reproduce their fabrics. If you look at them really closely, you will often notice that they are far from perfect. They were made from scraps. Little pieces of leftovers. Antique string quilts have seams that don't even meet, yet we love them anyway. They make interesting designs and have interesting fabrics. They are made of memories. They are made of leftovers; the things found lying around at the end of the day. Just like the fabrics in your scrap basket. These little pieces are your antiques (or they will be someday) and it's OK to put them together and make something beautiful and useful that is not quite perfect.

So, you now have all your scraps into piles to be strip pieced together and you're not quite sure what to do next. They are wrinkled and gnarled and some of them started out as 3-inch strips and make a wrong turn into 2¼-inches and then wobble back to 3¾-inches. How can you think about sewing these pieces together? They aren't even and getting them even would require you to press them nicely, attempt to fold them properly and line them up on a straight edge.

Don't do it. It isn't necessary. I know this doesn't follow the rules of any class you have ever taken or any book written, but I promise you that you can still sew them together. Lay the pieces right sides together as even as posiible, and just stitch. Pull the fabrics taut and don't worry about the wrinkles. SEW IN A STRAIGHT LINE. The strips will wave a little ... but it really doesn't matter as long as you aren't tempted to follow the curve. It's a scrap quilt. We will cut them into precise blocks later. If you leaf through the pages of this book and look at the designs you will see that the way the fabrics wiggle around really doesn't matter and adds character to the patterns. So stitch them together with reckless abandon.

Here are the rules that you should follow while piecing your strips:
* Make sure that you use at least a ¼-inch seam allowance when piecing your strips. You will be using the standard ¼-inch seam when piecing all the blocks as always but sometimes when you are piecing your strips you will find that in the middle of the piecing you run into a frayed spot and need to "take a bigger bite" out of the fabric to accommodate the variances in width. You can feel comfortable doing this because, again, the blocks will be cut to size after the strip piecing. It's more important that your seams stay together and the fabrics don't fray up to the seams.

*

- You should press your seams after every two to three strips. If you are a pressing genius, then you will be fine following what ever rule you like. In general, fabrics can start to "accordion" after three or more strips. It is not necessary to press your seams in any certain direction but if you prefer to do it that way go right ahead. I do prefer to press with starch. I feel this helps to keep the pieces nice and flat during cutting. Don't get concerned if your strips set begin to wobble and curve in another direction. This can happen when using pieces that are uneven. Try to make sure that your strip sets are pressed nicely. This will make the cutting process more accurate.
- The more fabric variation the better. Scrap quilts look best with many different fabrics, even if they are the same color tone. If some of your strips are wider than the others you can lay them on the cutting table and use a straight edge to trim them down. They DO NOT need to be a particular measurement so getting them "even" is not necessary. Just lay them down and cut them smaller (in half or thirds) and toss the remaining strips back into the pile for the next strip set.

Scrap basket on the cutting table.

Cutting Your Strip Sets Into Actual Blocks

Now that your strip sets are complete you can cut them into the necessary blocks for your chosen pattern. In some cases, you will be sewing together large triangles. They should be large enough that they won't give you any problems. Remember that you can always trim them and square them up when you are done because there are no points to cut off so don't worry if you think those pesky triangles will give you any trouble.

You will lay your ruler down on the strip sets as shown and cut out your pieces depending on the pattern you choose to make. If you own the triangle rulers mentioned earlier, and it's the correct size for the blocks you want to make, then you will be able to cut directly around the ruler and flip the ruler back and forth along the length of the strip until you can't cut anymore. You can save all the leftover ends if you like. Some may be able to be used in other patterns in the book. In *Crazy Signature Scraps and Crazy About Pinwheels* the blocks are made from leftover ends of the strips sets, extra small pieces in my scrap baskets and small leftover blocks or pieces of blocks that I made for other quilts. Each pattern indicates which shape and size to cut your pieces as well as how wide your strip sets should be before you begin cutting. However, if you are using a different ruler or different size ruler, you will need to make the necessary adjustments to your quilt blocks and fabric requirements.

At times, you will find that your strip sets will curl a little and not be completely straight. This is fine. They will be plenty wide enough to accommodate your pieces. You may find that you must shift your ruler around a little to make it fit. For instance, normally when cutting triangles out of a strip you would line the ruler up with the bottom edge of the strip and cut on both sides. Then take the ruler and flip and cut the next piece and so on. In the case of these pieces your strip sets will be a little larger than the width of your pieces. You will be able to flip the ruler back and forth to some degree but always realigning within the strip set to make sure the entire shape can be cut out properly.

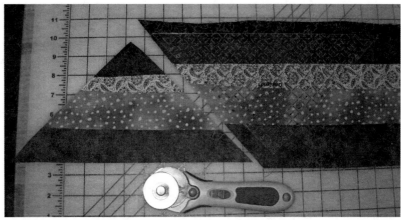
Flipping the triangle ruler on your strip set

15

How Not to Cut Your Hand Off

I have made a few assumptions in this book. After all, this is a book about using your scraps and so it could be assumed that you have made a few quilts in your time and have collected quite a few scraps. So I will also assume that you have learned rotary cutting safety. I know it's bad to assume, but I don't want to be responsible for imparting incorrect wisdom on the proper way to handle a rotary cutter.

On this subject, I really only have two things to say.
- Never use the rotary cutter in such a way that you are pushing towards your body or body parts. I know that some of us refuse to believe that we cannot cut in more than one direction. I admit that I have been guilty at times of using a rotary cutter improperly ... but even I have limits. You CAN pick up your pieces and turn them so that they are facing a safe cutting direction. When using the rulers, I often will cut two sides and then turn the project so that I can safely cut the third or fourth side. It is completely OK to lift and move your pieces.
- If you refuse to listen to the first direction and cut towards your hand or body please invest in a Kevlar™glove or something out of chain mail to prevent your loss of digits.

In all seriousness, please use extreme caution when cutting these pieces. I know that while making the quilts, I was excited and was in a big hurry to cut the pieces and put them up on the design wall. I may have, at times, rushed the cutting process just a little bit. That can be a very dangerous business. It only takes another minute to pick the pieces up and turn them on your cutting table so that you can safely cut them at a better angle. If you are one of those super quilters who is capable of cutting at any angle and you choose to go your own way, that's fine. I respect that ... and I applaud you for your ability (which I can still do because both of my hands are still attached). Please be careful and have fun.

Quilt Pattern Fabric Requirements

You will notice that the patterns give no real instruction for how much fabric to buy. I do give fabric requirements for border fabrics and supplementals (all the extra things that you need). For the scrap blocks, I only give you the number of finished cut pieces and not a yardage requirement. I know to some of you it may seem as though I am not giving enough information about fabric requirements. I assure you that you will need far fewer scraps to complete these projects than it seems. You will be able to cut quite a few blocks from each strip sets depending on the length of the strips and because I am not familiar with YOUR scraps I cannot give you exact measurements. I always seemed to have more blocks than I needed for each project.

If you reach a point that you just don't have the right colors in your scrap stash and you feel the need to supplement your scrap stash, you can make strips from your stash of regular fabrics or FQs. I would suggest cutting 2-inch strips (or something about that size) from your existing stash and adding it to your scraps. This seems to be about the right size within the blocks but anything can work. Keep in mind that using your stash for these violates what we are trying to accomplish in this book, but you have it as an option if you are not happy with your color choices.

I encourage you not to get frustrated or distracted by what seems like a lack of information. The most important thing is that you get into that scrap basket and sew. It won't be long before you have enough blocks for this quilt ... and you will have plenty more left over for a new project. So let's get stitching.

Measuring to Add the Borders to Your Quilts

I feel the need to insert this paragraph on adding borders even though you have probably already learned this. I normally add this paragraph to all my patterns just as a reminder. I felt the need to put it in the book for reference, but you can feel free to add your borders anyway that you wish. I will let you know that all measurements for border strips (which include their fabric requirements and cutting instructions) are calculated to be cut across the grain in strips. If you prefer to cut or tear your borders with the grain of the fabric you will need to adjust fabric requirements because you will need more yardage. The measurements of each quilt center are found throughout the pattern so you should be able to tell the yardage measurements that you need in inches if you decide to make your borders another way.

Before adding the borders to your quilt, measure the quilt width and length of the quilt top at the mid-point of each edge (in case the outer edges have stretched). After sewing the strips together, be sure to cut the border strips to the exact width and length of the quilt top before adding them to the quilt top. This will prevent rippling and ensure that the quilt top lays flat. If you start measuring the quilt to add the top and bottom borders first, be sure to re-measure the quilt in the opposite direction before cutting the side borders.

Terminology

WOF - Width of Fabric
FQ - Fat Quarter
Unplanned Project - Scrap project using random strips of fabric with no color or tone distinction.
Color Organized Project - Scrap project with color and tone distribution before the stitching process.

The Quilts

Hidden Hexies
Sample size is 45-inches x 62-inches
Pattern found on Page 28

Easy Diamond Delight
Sample size is 42-inches x 65-inches
Pattern found on Page 30

Crazy Signature Scraps
Sample size is 46-inches x 62-inches
Pattern found on Page 32

ZigZag Pizzazz
Sample size is 60-inches x 82-inches
Pattern found on Page 35

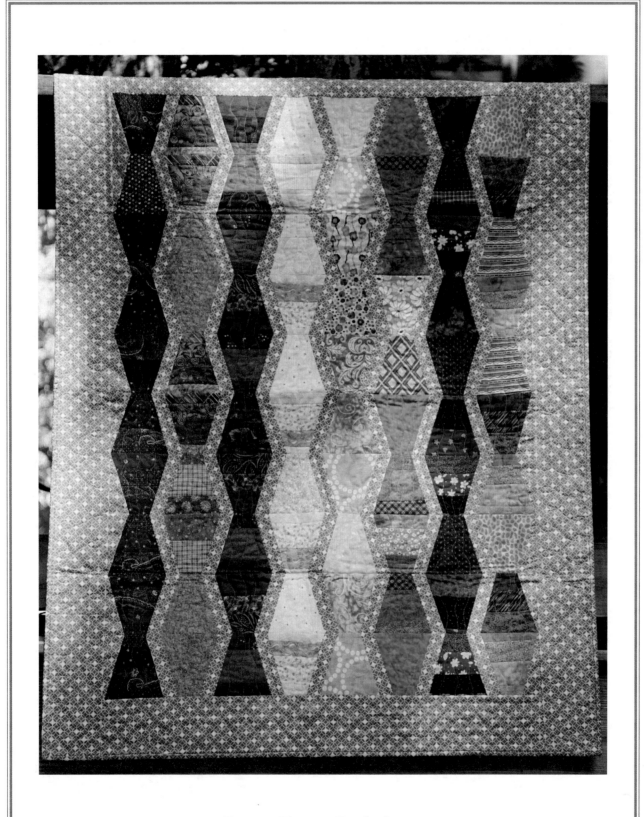

EvenFlow Rainbow
Sample size is 40-inches x 50-inches
Pattern found on Page 37

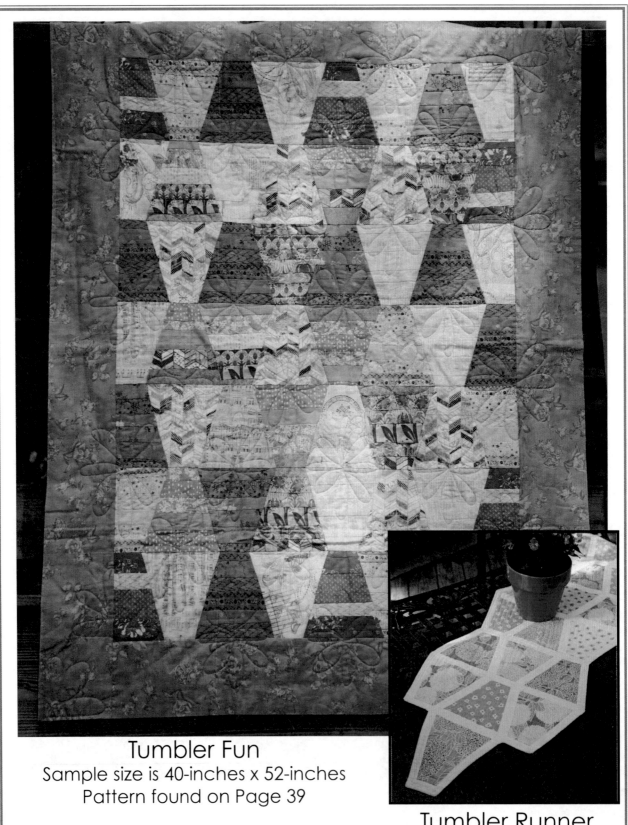

Tumbler Fun
Sample size is 40-inches x 52-inches
Pattern found on Page 39

Tumbler Runner
17-inches x 55-inches
Pattern found on Page 41

Diamond Play
Sample size is 50-inches x 68-inches
Pattern found on Page 44

Crazy About Pinwheels
Sample size is 44-inches x 60-inches
Pattern found on Page 47

The Patterns

Hidden Hexies
45-inches x 62-inches

P. 19

P. 19

Notes: For this quilt I chose to put strips together based on tone. I wanted solid pieces of color so when I mixed them they would look scrappy but not too scrappy. This gives the quilt the illusion of being constructed of solid pieces. In some cases the triangles are solid pieces if I have a piece of scrap large enough to cut out one shape. The "hidden hexies" are made from turning the triangles in such a way that circle is formed. Mix the blocks together and spread out the hexies so they don't overlap each other.

Tools Used:
6 ½-inch 60° Triangle or CWQ Template 60T6 Triangle

~

Scrap Blocks Needed:
120 Scrap Triangles. Make sure that you have at least a few groups of 6 of the same color for the hidden "hexies". My quilt has 8 "hexies".

~

Supplemental Fabric Requirements:
Border Fabric : 1¼ yards

Optional Binding : ½ yard

~

Border Cutting Instructions:
From Border Fabric:
• Cut 6½-inches x WOF strips

Note* If you adjust the size of the quilt, you will need to adjust the Border Fabric and Binding measurements and calculate the number of fabric strips needed for the border.

Step 1: Making Your Strip Sets
Decide the scrap strips you intend to use for this project and make your horizontal strip sets. Strips should be slightly larger than 6½-inches (the height of the 6-inch triangle, or if using a different ruler, larger than the height of the ruler.) If you make the strip sets too big you will create more waste.

Step 2: Creating Your Blocks From Your Strip Sets
After pressing your strip sets, lay them on your cutting table and begin cutting with your triangle ruler as shown. You will be using the entire triangle so you can trim all the way around your ruler, or for safety sake, cut two sides of the angle and then lift and reposition the fabric. Square up after one or two triangles to allow for the unruly strips. Cut as many triangles from your strip sets as possible or until you reach 120.

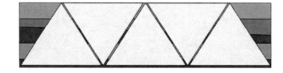

Step3: Assembling Your Quilt Top
Lay your blocks out on your table or design wall in a setting that is pleasing to you. Use the quilt diagram as a reference for making your "hidden hexies".

The quilt will be sewn together in rows of triangles. Triangles are sewn side to side (matching the points with no offset) and will create a nice straight edge on the top and bottom of each row.

Once all the rows have been assembled, layer the rows together and carefully pin each seam so the triangle points don't shift while sewing. You will save yourself a lot of heartache if you pin your seams prior to sewing.

Step 4: Trimming the Sides of the Quilt
Once the quilt center is assembled, you will notice that the sides are not straight. You can choose to leave each point on the side of the quilt and finish the quilt with a sawtooth edge.

If you are interested in adding a border, you will need to trim the sides of the quilt straight. To do this lay the quilt top out flat on your cutting mat. Using your longest quilting ruler, lay the ruler along the side of the quilt with the ¼-inch line along the seam allowance in the blocks. Trim the side of the quilt at the ¼-inch seam allowance making certain that you do not cut off the seam allowance. This will ensure that the seam of the border falls right at the tips of the triangles. Trim both sides before adding the borders.

Step 5: Adding the Borders
I give tips in the beginning of the book about adding borders to your quilts. You may choose to change the size of this quilt so I will not give instructions on the number of strips to use.
The borders on the sample of this quilt are made from 6½-inch strips. Measure the sides of your quilt and cut the strips according to length. After attaching the strips to the sides of the quilt, re-measure the quilt for the border strips on the top and bottom of the quilt top.

Easy Diamond Delight
42-inches x 65-inches

P. 90

Notes: I used some of my leftover scrap strip sets to make this quilt. I alternated the lights and darks to make a traditional scrap quilt design. I did mix my lights and darks in some of the blocks. So you can do your diamonds out of a color tone or you could make this quilt completely scrappy. You can see in some of the background triangles I used solid pieces and some are strip pieced. You can make your whole quilt either way. I would love to remake this one with random scraps because it would look equally awesome. This is by far the easiest way to make a diamond quilt. There are no 45° seams to meet and it is much easier to get your points perfect. If you are interested in making a diamond quilt from diamonds and not triangles we have a template for that too... and the pattern is in our first book All Scrapped Out!

Tools Used:
6½-inch 60° Triangle or CWQ Template 60T6 Triangle
~
Scrap Blocks Needed:
50 Scrap Triangles of Color
44 Scrap Triangles of Background
~
Supplemental Fabric Requirements:
Border Fabric : 1 ¼ yards
Optional Binding : ½ yard
~
Border Cutting Instructions:
From Border Fabric:
• Cut 6 - 6½-inches x WOF strips

Note* If you adjust the size of the quilt, you will need to adjust the Border Fabric and Binding measurements and calculate the number of fabric strips needed for the border.

Step 1: Making Your Strip Sets
Decide the scrap strips you intend to use for this project and make your horizontal strip sets. Strips should be slightly larger than 6½-inches (the height of the 6-inch triangle, or if using a different ruler, larger than the height of the ruler.) If you make the strip sets too big you will create more waste.

Step 2: Creating Your Blocks From Your Strip Sets
After pressing your strip sets, lay them on your cutting table and begin cutting with your triangle ruler as shown. You will be using the entire triangle so you can trim all the way around your ruler, or for safety sake, cut two sides of the angle and then lift and reposition the fabric. Square up after one or two triangles to allow for the unruly strips. Cut as many triangles from your strip sets as possible or until you reach 50 blocks of color and 44 blocks of background.

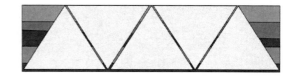

Step 3: Assembling the Quilt Top
Lay your blocks out on your table or design wall in a setting that is pleasing to you. Use the quilt diagram as a reference for making your diamonds.
The quilt will be sewn together in rows of triangles. Triangles are sewn side to side (matching the points with no offset) and will create a nice straight edge on the top and bottom of each row.

Once all the rows have been assembled, layer the rows together and carefully pin each seam so the triangle points don't shift while sewing. You will save yourself a lot of heartache if you pin your seams prior to sewing.

Step 4: Trimming the Sides of the Quilt
Once the quilt center is assembled, you will notice that the sides are not straight. You can choose to leave each point on the side of the quilt and finish the quilt with a sawtooth edge.

If you are interested in adding a border, you will need to trim the sides of the quilt straight. To do this lay the quilt top out flat on your cutting mat. Using your longest quilting ruler, lay the ruler along the side of the quilt with the ¼-inch line along the seam allowance in the blocks. Trim the side of the quilt at the ¼-inch seam allowance making certain that you do not cut off the seam allowance. This will ensure that the seam of the border falls right at the tips of the triangles. Trim both sides before adding the borders.

Step 5: Adding the Borders
I give tips in the beginning of the book about adding borders to your quilts. You may choose to change the size of this quilt so I will not give instructions on the number of strips to use.
The borders on the sample of this quilt are made from 6½-inch strips. Measure the sides of your quilt and cut the strips according to length. After attaching the strips to the sides of the quilt, re-measure the quilt for the border strips on the top and bottom of the quilt top.

Crazy Signature Scraps
46-inches x 62-inches

p. 91

Notes: This quilt was super fun. I love signature quilts and sashing on point. This quilt looks very traditional but the blocks are made from all the leftover bits. I chose to divide my bits by color and tone. However, this is another quilt that would look amazing if you just used your little bits of random colors from the bottom of your bin. Make your crazy quilt blocks and then slash them diagonally. I would also like this quilt with a smaller sashing (1½-inches). If you are a modern/contemporary quilter, think about making this one with a slash method. Assemble the block, slash it with a straight edge and then add your strip wherever you want. You can make the whole block look like a snowflake for winter.

Tools Used:
Standard Square Ruler, Standard Rectangle 24-inches

~

Scrap Blocks Needed:
24 - 6½-inch crazy blocks

~

Supplemental Fabric Requirements:
Sashing and Border #1 Fabric : 1¼ yards
Border #2 Fabric : 1 yard
Optional Binding : ½ yard

~

Border and Sashing Cutting Instructions:
From Fabric:
- Cut 6 - 5½-inches x WOF strips for Border #2
- Cut 5 - 2½-inches x WOF strips for Border #1. One strip will be cut in half and used for each side.
- Cut 2 -12½-inch x WOF strips for sashing. From thesee cut:
-      Cut 24 - 2½-inch x 12½-inch sashing strips

Note* If you adjust the size of the quilt, you will need to adjust the Border Fabric and Binding measurements and calculate the number of fabric strips needed for the border.

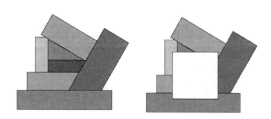

When your mass of scraps gets bigger than 6½-inches square, take it to the cutting table and trim it to size. Repeat this process and make 24 blocks (or enough to make the size quilt you are looking for). You can cut the blocks to a larger size if you would like but I have found from experience that 6 or 7-inches is a really nice size.

Step 2: Finishing the Blocks
Once your crazy blocks are complete, lay them on your cutting table and use a straight edge to cut them apart diagonally from corner to corner as shown making two triangles.

Step 1: Creating the Crazy Blocks
Using all the leftover fabric pieces from cutting your strip sets and random pieces of fabric you have lying around, start sewing fabrics together to create something resembling near a square. There really is no rhyme or reason to how these blocks go together. One option is to start with two clean cut angles leftover from some of your strip sets and stitch them together. You can trim using a straight edge on one side and then begin attaching random pieces (such as strips that were too small for your strip sets, leftover corners and such.) Rotate you block after adding each piece to make it visually interesting on all sides. Another option is to start with a block or block piece from another quilt and then build up around it on the sides.

Fold each triangle in half point to point and press or finger press to make a crease for reference.

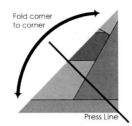

Fold one 2½-inch x 12½-inch sashing strip end to end and make a center crease.

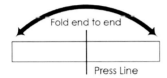

Place the sashing strip on the long side of the triangle matching the center creases, pin and sew right sides together. Press and then add the other triangle to the other side of the sashing strip. Match the center creases, pin and sew right sides together. Press.

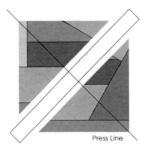

When both triangles are attached to the sashing strip, trim the block square. Repeat and make 24 blocks.

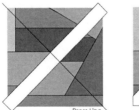

Step 3: Assembling the Quilt Top
Lay your blocks out on your table or design wall in a setting that is pleasing to you. Use the quilt diagram as a reference for making your diamonds. The quilt will be sewn together in rows.

Once all the rows have been assembled, layer the rows together and carefully pin each seam so the block seams don't shift while sewing. You will save yourself a lot of heartache if you pin your seams prior to sewing.

Step 4: Adding the Outer Sashing (Border #1)
I give tips in the beginning of the book about adding borders to your quilts. You may choose to change the size of this quilt so I will not give instructions on the number of strips to use.

The borders on the sample of this quilt are made from 2½-inch strips. Measure the sides of your quilt and cut the strips according to length. After attaching the strips to the sides of the quilt, re-measure the quilt for the border strips on the top and bottom of the quilt top.

Step 5: Adding the Outer Borders.
The borders on the sample of this quilt are made from 6½-inch strips. Measure the sides of your quilt and cut the strips according to length. After attaching the strips to the sides of the quilt, re-measure the quilt for the border strips on the top and bottom of the quilt top.

Zig Zag Pizzazz
60-inches x 82-inches

Notes: This quilt was made from some of the larger pieces from my stash, some fabric samples and scrap strip sets. My modern fabrics tend to be larger pieces so I was able to get a few triangles cut from each piece. The backgrounds are all solids. I like making chevrons from strip set though because the seams give the quilt real direction. Most people don't put cornerstones on a modern quilt but I did not have enough of the border print to mitre the corners and I definitely wanted a border. You could leave the border off or choose something else. You can also make this quilt completely scrappy as well. Separate your colors or mix them up. You can also add more color and put your chevrons right next to each other. Have fun with it.

Tools Used:
6½-inch 90° Triangle ruler or CWQ Templates 90T6 Triangle

~

Scrap Blocks Needed:
96 - 6½-inch half-square triangle blocks (48 scrap triangles)
4 - 6½-inch cornerblocks for border.

~

Supplemental Fabric Requirements:
Background Fabric: $1^1/_3$ yards
Border Fabric : 1½ yards (just in case)
Optional Binding : ¾ yard

~

Background and Border Cutting Instructions:
From the Background Fabric:
• Cut 7 - 6½-inches x WOF strips. From these strips:
• Cut 48 - 6½-inch triangles.
From Border Fabric:
• Cut 8 - 6½-inches x WOF strips

Note* If you adjust the size of the quilt, you will need to adjust the Border Fabric and Binding measurements and calculate the number of fabric strips needed for the border.

Step 2: Creating Your Blocks From Your Strip Sets
After pressing your strip sets, lay them on your cutting table and begin cutting with your triangle ruler as shown. Cut two sides of the angle and then lift and reposition the fabric. Square up after one or two triangles to allow for the unruly strips. Cut as many triangles from your strip sets as possible or until you reach 48.

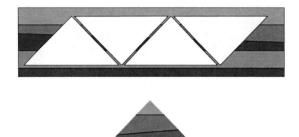

Step 1: Making Your Strip Sets
Decide the scrap strips you intend to use for this project and make your horizontal strip sets. Strips should be slightly larger than 6½-inches (the height of the 6-inch triangle, or if using a different ruler, larger than the height of the ruler.) If you make the strip sets too big you will create more waste.

Step 3: Assembling the Blocks
To complete the blocks, layer one scrap triangle with one background triangle from the cutting instructions, right sides together and sew together on the long diagonal. Open and press to create one half-square triangle block. Repeat this process and make 96 blocks.

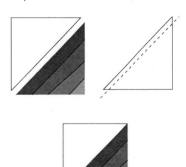

Step 4: Assembling the Quilt Top

Lay your blocks out in a setting that is pleasing to the eye with the background blocks in alternating direction using the quilt diagram as a reference. The quilt will sewn together in rows. Once all the rows have been assembled, layer the rows together and carefully pin each seam so the block seams don't shift while sewing. You will save yourself a lot of heartache if you pin your seams prior to sewing.

Step 5: Adding the Borders

I give tips in the beginning of the book about adding borders to your quilts. You may choose to change the size of this quilt so I will not give instructions on the number of strips to use.

The borders on the sample of this quilt are made from 6½-inch strips. Measure the sides of your quilt and cut the strips according to length. After attaching the strips to the sides of the quilt, re-measure the quilt for the border strips on the top and bottom of the quilt top. For this quilt I added cornerstones due to the length of border fabric I had left. If you also wish to add the cornerstones, you will add your 6½-inch squares to the ends of each side strip.

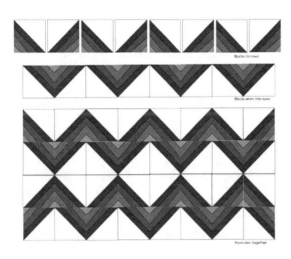

Blocks in rows

Blocks sewn into rows

Rows sew together

EvenFlow Rainbow
40-inches x 50-inches

Notes: The Tumbler is my new favorite template and I currently make one in three sizes. There are so many possibilities with this block. In this quilt I decided to use up all the leftover charm squares I had lying around and used the CWQ-TRAPCH charm tumbler. I decided to add sashing between the colored rows but you can leave out the sashing completely if you would like. You can also sash each block (like I did with Tumbler Runner in this book). In some cases I did not have enough charm square to complete a color so I used my trusty scrap strip sets again. You could even cut this template from your crazy blocks. for the edge of the quilt I added a row of background tumblers and used my ruler to trim the edge. It's all up to you.

Tools Used:
5-inch Tumbler for Charm Square or CWQ Templates
TRAPCH Charm Tumbler

~

Scrap Blocks Needed:
10 Blocks from each color of the Rainbow (8 colors in quilt)

~

Supplemental Fabric Requirements:
Sashing Fabric: 1 yard
Border Fabric : ¾ yard
Optional Binding : ½ yard

~

Sashing and Border Cutting Instructions:
From Sashing Fabric:
* Cut 3 - 6-inches x WOF strips. From those strips:
*   Cut 70 - 1½-inch x 6-inch rectangles
* Cut 2 - 5-inch x WOF strips. From these strips
*   Cut 20 - 5-inch Tumbler blocks for the sides.
From Border Fabric:
*   Cut 6 - 4½-inches x WOF strips

Note* If you adjust the size of the quilt, you will need to adjust the Border Fabric and Binding measurements and calculate the number of fabric strips needed for the border.

Step 1: Making Your Strip Sets
Decide the scrap strips you intend to use for this project and make your horizontal strip sets. Strips should be slightly larger than 5½-inches (the height of the 5-inch tumbler, or if using a different ruler, larger than the height of the ruler.) If you make the strip sets too big you will create more waste.

Step 2: Creating Your Blocks From Your Strip Sets
After pressing your strip sets, lay them on your cutting table and begin cutting with your tumbler template as shown. Cut two sides of the angle and then lift and reposition the fabric. Square up after one or two tumblers to allow for the unruly strips. You can trim the strip to the height of the ruler if this makes cutting easier for you. Cut as many tumblers from your strip sets or charm sqaures as possible or until you make 80 blocks (10 of each color.)

Step 3: Assembling the Quilt Top
You will assemble the quilt top in rows using the quilt diagram as a reference. Begin and end each row with one tumbler block cut from the sashing fabric. Sew one sashing/border tumbler to the first color, right sides together and press. Then add a sashing strip, right sides together and press.

Square up the row and trim the ends of the sashing and then move on to the next block in the row. This will help ensure that ensure that your rows are straight. You will offset the blocks in the seam by ¼-inch before sewing the seam.

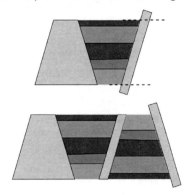

Following the photo and the diagram, the rows are assembled in this order: background, red, pink, orange, yellow, green, blue, indigo, violet. Once all the rows have been assembled, layer the rows together and carefully pin each seam so the tumbler and sashing seams don't shift while sewing. You will save yourself a lot of heartache if you pin your seams prior to sewing.

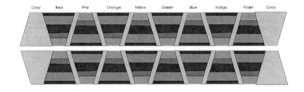

Step 4: Trimming the Sides of the Quilt
Once the quilt center is assembled, you will notice that the sides are not straight. You can choose to leave each point on the side of the quilt and finish the quilt with a sawtooth edge. If you are interested in adding a border, you will need to trim the sides of the quilt straight. Lay the quilt top out flat on your cutting mat. Using your longest quilting ruler, lay the ruler along the side of the quilt with the ¼-inch line along the seam allowance in the blocks. Trim the side of the quilt at the ¼-inch seam allowance making certain that you do not cut off the seam allowance. This will ensure that the seam of the border falls right at the tips of the tumblers. Trim both sides before adding the borders.

Step 5: Adding the Borders
I give tips in the beginning of the book about adding borders to your quilts. You may choose to change the size of this quilt so I will not give instructions on the number of strips to use.
The borders on the sample of this quilt are made from 4½-inch strips. Measure the sides of your quilt and cut the strips according to length. After attaching the strips to the sides of the quilt, re-measure the quilt for the border strips on the top and bottom of the quilt top.

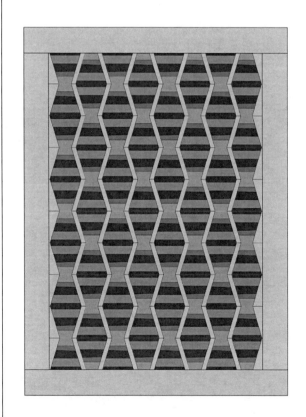

Tumbler Fun
40-inches x 52-inches

Notes: Here is another tumbler quilt. This one is made with our CWQ-TRAP6 Tumbler template. The template is 6½-inches and the perfect size to work with your scrap strips. In some cases when I had a particularly decorative scrap from these fabric samples I would cut a solid block. However, most of the blocks in this quilt are assembled from scraps. This is another perfect quilt to be made with random scraps of fabric. You can used large pieces for a solid block or sew lots of random strips together. You can alternate colors. The layout is virtually the same as the previous quilt in this book without a sashing. You can even put several blocks the same color together. I love the size of this block. This one would also be perfect for crazy blocks. So many possibilities are available to suit your needs. At the time of production our template was the largest on the market and would be perfect used with fat quarters and jelly rolls as well.

Tools Used:
6½-inch Tumbler for Charm Square or CWQ Templates
TRAPCH Charm Tumbler

~

Scrap Blocks Needed:
56 Scrap Blocks

~

Supplemental Fabric Requirements:
Border Fabric : 1¼ yards
Optional Binding : ½ yard

~

Border Cutting Instructions:
From Border Fabric:
•   Cut 6 - 6½-inches x WOF strips

Note* If you adjust the size of the quilt, you will need to adjust the Border Fabric and Binding measurements and calculate the number of fabric strips needed for the border.

Step 1: Making Your Strip Sets

Decide the scrap strips you intend to use for this project and make your horizontal strip sets. Strips should be slightly larger than 6½-inches (the height of the 6½-inch tumbler, or if using a different ruler, larger than the height of the ruler.) If you make the strip sets too big you will create more waste.

Step 2: Creating Your Blocks From Your Strip Sets

After pressing your strip sets, lay them on your cutting table and begin cutting with your tumbler template as shown. Cut two sides of the angle and then lift and reposition the fabric. Square up after one or two tumblers to allow for the unruly strips. You can trim the strip to the height of the ruler if this makes cutting easier for you. Cut as many tumblers from your strip sets or charm sqaures as possible or until you make 56 blocks.

Step 3: Assembling the Quilt Top

You will assemble the quilt top in rows using the quilt diagram as a reference. Lay two tumblers right sides together. You will offset the blocks in the seam by ¼-inch before sewing the seam. Sew together and press.

Once all the rows have been assembled, layer the rows together and carefully pin each seam so the tumbler and sashing seams don't shift while sewing. You will save yourself a lot of heartache if you pin your seams prior to sewing.

Step 4: Trimming the Sides of the Quilt

Once the quilt center is assembled, you will notice that the sides are not straight. You can choose to leave each point on the side of the quilt and finish the quilt with a sawtooth edge. If you are interested in adding a border, you will need to trim the sides of the quilt straight. Lay the quilt top out flat on your cutting mat. Using your longest quilting ruler, lay the ruler along the side of the quilt with the ¼-inch line along the seam allowance in the blocks. Trim the side of the quilt at the ¼-inch seam allowance making certain that you do not cut off the seam allowance. This will ensure that the seam of the border falls right at the tips of the tumblers. Trim both sides before adding the borders.

Step 5: Adding the Borders

I give tips in the beginning of the book about adding borders to your quilts. You may choose to change the size of this quilt so I will not give instructions on the number of strips to use.

The borders on the sample of this quilt are made from 6½-inch strips. Measure the sides of your quilt and cut the strips according to length. After attaching the strips to the sides of the quilt, re-measure the quilt for the border strips on the top and bottom of the quilt top.

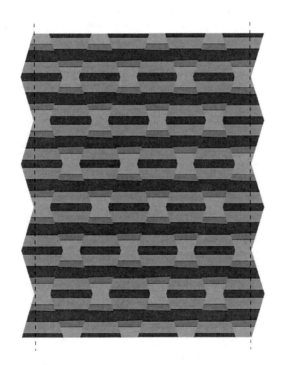

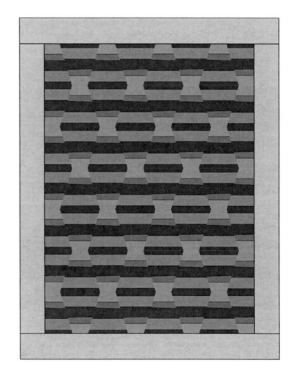

Tumbler Runner
17-inches x 55-inches

Notes: This is an adorable and unique table runner made from 20 tumbler blocks. I had some scraps of a line of Moda fabrics left and choose to make this bright little number with white sashing. I like the edges of this table runner. Based on all the edges I used the quick turn method instead of using a traditional binding on all those edges. It works perfectly. Try this with the leftovers from your next fat quater pack. The runner can be made to any size to suit you.

Tools Used:
6½-inch Tumbler or CWQ Templates TRAP6 Tumbler

~

Scrap Blocks Needed:
20 Scrap Tumblers

~

Supplemental Fabric Requirements:
Sashing Fabric: ¾ yard
Optional Binding: ½ yard. *Not a conventional binding.*
I recommend completing this table runner by using the "quick turn" method as indicated in the pattern. For this method you do not need to purchase the binding fabric.

~

Sashing Cutting Instructions
Cut 4 - 1½-inch x WOF. From those strips cut:
    Cut 3 - 1½-inches x 20-inches
    Cut 4 - 1½-inches x 15-inches
    Cut 2 - 1½-inches x 5-inches
Cut 2 - 9-inch x WOF strips. From those strips cut:
    Cut 28 - 1½-inches x 9-inches.

~

Note* If you adjust the size of the quilt, you will need to adjust the Border Fabric and Binding measurements and calculate the number of fabric strips needed for the border.

Step 1: Making Your Strip Sets
I made all my tumblers in this runner from solid pieces but, if you are using scrap strips sets, decide the scrap strips you intend to use for this project and make your horizontal strip sets. Strips should be slightly larger than 6½-inches (the height of the 6½-inch tumbler, or if using a different ruler, larger than the height of the ruler.) If you make the strip sets too big you will create more waste.

Step 2: Creating Your Blocks From Your Strip Sets
After pressing your strip sets, lay them on your cutting table and begin cutting with your tumbler template as shown. Cut two sides of the angle and then lift and reposition the fabric. Square up after one or two tumblers to allow for the unruly strips. You can trim the strip to the height of the ruler if this makes cutting easier for you. Cut as many tumblers from your strip sets or charm sqaures as possible or until you make 20 blocks.

Step 3: Assembling the Quilt Top
You will assemble the quilt top in rows using the quilt diagram as a reference. Begin and end each row with one 1½-inch x 9-inch sashing strip cut from the sashing fabric. Sew one sashing strip to the first tumbler in the row, right sides together and press. Then add a sashing strip, right sides together and press. Square up the row and trim the ends of the sashing and then move on to the next block in the row. This will help ensure that ensure that your rows are straight. You will offset the blocks in the seam by ¼-inch before sewing the seam.

Once all the rows have been assembled, layer the rows together with the remaining longer sashing strips and carefully pin each seam so the tumbler and sashing seams don't shift while sewing. You can use the fold and press technique (illustrated on pg. 33) to find the center of each row and strips so you leave yourself plenty of room to square up on either side of the runner. Do not trim the end of the rows in the corners until you have the whole top completed. You will save yourself a lot of heartache if you pin your seams prior to sewing.

Trim your sashing strips by measuring the center of the point and leave a pencil marking. Then use your rotary cutter and a straight edge or your scissors and clipping the excess.

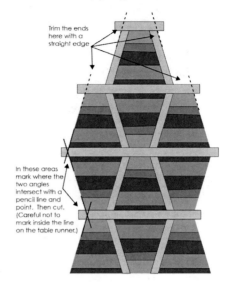

Trim the ends here with a straight edge

In these areas mark where the two angles intersect with a pencil line and point. Then cut. (Careful not to mark inside the line on the table runner.)

Be sure to add the final 1½-inch by 5-inch sashing strips to both ends of the runner. Once the runner is complete you can trim and square all the raw edges.

Step 4: Finishing the Project
Your project is now ready to be quilted and bound. I decided that the simplest way to finish this quilt was not to make a traditional binding. There were simply too many corners for me.

Instead try cutting a larger backing and batting piece. Layer the quilt top and backing right sides together on your table. Then lay the batting on top of those pieces. Sew all the way around the runner top with ¼-inch seam (or whatever is comfortable) and leave an opening of at least 6-8 inches between the start and stop point. The diagram shows to leave an opening between the dots.

Once you have completed the sewing, trim around the seam leaving ¼-inch seam allowance. Clip down any bulky points and corners being careful not to catch your stitches. Put your hand into the opening in the seam and pull the runner right side out.
In the diagram at right, note that the layers show as the runner top (wrong side up) as the first layer, right sides together with the runner backing. The bottom layer is the batting. After you have sewn all the way around the runner you can trim the excess with a rotary cutter or scissors.

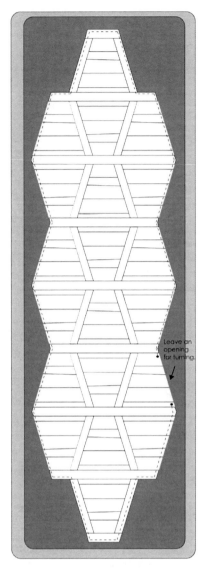

Leave an opening for turning.

A view of the finished product with the quilting.

You will need to poke all the corners with a tool or the eraser tip of a pencil to get those crisp, clean points and corners. If you find that the corners aren't looking perfect you may need to clip in more places or trim out some bulk. Once the runner is how you like it, press with an iron. I also like to use a little starch.

When nice and flat, top stitch around the outside edge of the runner, careful to push the seam allowance into the open seam so that the runner closes when finished. You can also use a little fusible stabilizer or seam glue to hold the seam closed while you top stitch.

Then quilt the runner as desired. I chose some straight line quilting to finish this project and it turned out great.

Diamond Play
50-inches x 68-inches

Notes: This quilt is by far one of my favorites. It has so much color in it and it's made from so many memories. It also begins and ends in multiple places. That is not typical for me. I like perfect grids. I am a huge fan of symmetry. So this was my challenge to myself. Of course it takes on the fabric look of a more traditional quilt because it is made entirely of scrap strips and the ghosts of quilts past. I can only imagine what yours will look like. You can choose any fabrics you would like. You can make this completely from random scraps. I think the look would be really interesting. Perhaps you would like colors more closely resembling a rainbow for the prism effect. You can also use solid pieced instead of strip sets if you have enough. The instructions include a lettered diagram so you know how many of each color triangles to make to get my pattern effect. If you choose a different pattern you are on your own. Copy the diagram and use your pencils to color it in or use your favorite quilt design software. It is super fun to come up with your own design.

Tools Used:
6½-inch 90° Triangle Ruler or CWQ Templates 90T6 Triangle.

~

Scrap Blocks Needed:
140 half-square triangle blocks total. Follow the quilt diagram color chart to figure the number of each colored triangles.

~

Supplemental Fabric Requirements:
Border Fabric : 1¼ yards.
Optional Binding : ½ yard

~

Border Cutting Instructions:
From Border Fabric:
* Cut 8 - 5-inches x WOF strips

Note* If you adjust the size of the quilt, you will need to adjust the Border Fabric and Binding measurements and calculate the number of fabric strips needed for the border.

Step 1: Making Your Strip Sets
Decide the scrap strips you intend to use for this project and make your horizontal strip sets. Strips should be slightly larger than 6½-inches (the height of the 6-inch triangle, or if using a different ruler, larger than the height of the ruler.) If you make the strip sets too big you will create more waste.

Step 2: Creating Your Triangles From Your Strips
After pressing your strip sets, lay them on your cutting table and begin cutting with your triangle ruler as shown. Cut two sides of the angle and then lift and reposition the fabric. Square up after one or two triangles to allow for the unruly strips. You can trim the strip to the height of the ruler if this makes cutting easier for you. Cut as many triangles from your strip sets as possible or until you reach 140. *See diagram on page 46 for reference to how many triangles of each color.

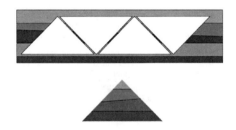

Step 3: Creating Your Blocks
Following the quilt diagram, lay out your triangles on a design wall for the proper placement of colors to create your diamonds. Once your triangles are laid out in the proper places you will need to sew each block together into a half square triangle.

The quilt diagram shows the triangles paired together to make half-square triangles. One color attaches to the next color group. Start with the corner of the quilt and take the first two triangles, lay right sides together and stitch on the long side. Press and square the block. Then repeat that process until all the triangles are assembled together. You will now have 70 completed blocks.

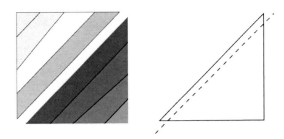

For additional reference, I have provided a diagram on the last page of this pattern for each triangle in this quilt. If you make the quilt exactly by the pattern, the diagram will tell you exactly how many triangles of each color you will need to complete the pattern. Check the corresponding letter in the diagram.

Step 4: Assembling Your Quilt Top
Once all of the blocks are assembled and are back on the design wall. You can begin assembling the rows of the quilt. Be sure to maintain the direction of the squares so your finished rows look the way you intended in your quilt diagram. The stitch all the rows together into the quilt top.

Step 5: Adding the Borders
I give tips in the beginning of the book about adding borders to your quilts. You may choose to change the size of this quilt so I will not give instructions on the number of strips to use.
The borders on the sample of this quilt are made from 5-inch strips. Measure the sides of your quilt and cut the strips according to length. After attaching the strips to the sides of the quilt, re-measure the quilt for the border strips on the top and bottom of the quilt top.

Triangles to
cut for each
diamond:

A - 4
B - 10
C - 12
D - 13
E - 6
F - 2
G - 2
H - 2
I - 19
J - 5
K - 3
L - 1
M - 17
N - 16
O - 14
P - 10
Q - 4

Crazy About Pinwheels
44-inches x 60-inches

Notes: This is absolutely my favorite quilt in the book because it's my "free" quilt. The pinwheel blocks are made from leftover jelly roll strip sets from another quilt. I used the leftover border and backing of the quilt and cut floral square. All the leftover snipits went into the 4 crazy blocks. Then I put the pinwheels blocks togther and then used all the other fabrics to fill in the spaces. A little bit of complimentary fabric for a border and BOOM... free quilt made from leftovers. You can add extra blocks to your quilt. Don't be afraid to cut up leftover borders and trim leftover blocks down and make something new. When I put the two quilt side by side made from the same fabrics they look complimentary but totally different. This is a great idea if you are making a quilt for your bed and have lots leftover. Think about using those leftovers to make a compimentary throw for those chillier nights. Most importantly... have great fun with it.

Tools Used:
6½-inch 90° Triangle Ruler or CWQ Templates 90T6 Triangle

~

Scrap Blocks Needed:
36 Half-square triangles of colors for Pinwheels
36 Half-square triangles of backgrounds for Pinwheels or see optional background fabrics.
14 Floral Blocks 6½-inches
4 Crazy Quilt Blocks 6½-inches

~

Supplemental Fabric Requirements:
Background Fabric for Pinwheels: 1¼ yards
Border Fabric : ¾ yard
Optional Binding : ½ yard

~

Border Cutting Instructions:
From Border Fabric:
• Cut 8 - 4½-inches x WOF strips

Note* If you adjust the size of the quilt, you will need to adjust the Border Fabric and Binding measurements and calculate the number of fabric strips needed for the border.

Step 1: Making Your Strip Sets

Decide the scrap strips you intend to use for this project and make your horizontal strip sets. Strips should be slightly larger than 6½-inches (the height of the 6-inch triangle, or if using a different ruler, larger than the height of the ruler.) If you make the strip sets too big you will create more waste.

Step 2: Creating the Pinwheel Blocks from strips

After pressing your strip sets, lay them on your cutting table and begin cutting with your triangle ruler as shown. Cut two sides of the angle and then lift and reposition the fabric. Square up after one or two triangles to allow for the unruly strips. Cut as many triangles from your strip sets as possible. If you are following this pattern cut 36 triangles. If you want your pinwheels blocks to be made of all the same colorway remember to cut 4 strips of each color.

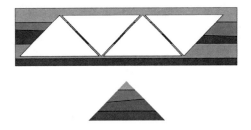

Once all of your colored triangles have been cut you can attached them to your triangles of background right sides together. Sew together on the long side and press. You should now have 36 half square triangles.

Following the block diagram, layer the 4 blocks of each color together to create your pinwheels. Repeat this process and make 9 pinwheel blocks.

Step 3: Creating the Crazy Blocks
Using all of the leftover fabric pieces from cutting your strip sets and random pieces of fabric you have lying around in the same color family, start sewing fabrics together to create something resembling a square. There really is no rhyme or reason to how these blocks go together.

One option is to start with two clean cut angles left over from some of your strip sets and stitch them together using their longest sides. You can trim them using a straight edge on one side and then begin attaching random pieces (such as strips that were too small for your strip sets, leftover corners, and such.) Rotate your block after adding each piece to make it visually interesting on all sides.

Another option is to begin with a block or block piece from another quilt and then build up around it on the sides. Once your block is large enough, trim all sides to a 6½-inch square.

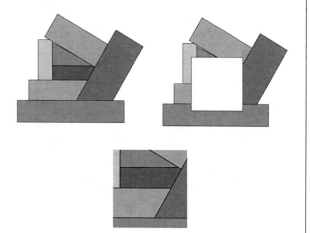

Step 4: Creating the Fill-In Blocks.
For the fill-in blocks on this quilt, I used leftover pieces of Border print from my other quilt. I trimmed all fabrics into 6½-inch squares and added them to my block pile. You could also sew two pieces of fabric together to make a single sqaure depending on the size of your leftovers. For this quilt you will need 14 squares.

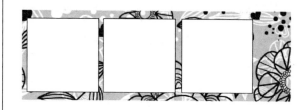

Step 5: Assembling the Quilt Top
Following the quilt diagram, you will lay all the blocks out on your design wall until the block placement is pleasing to the eye. In some cases you will have two squares next to each other that will be sewn into a rectangle. We did not cut them as rectangles because the squares give you more flexibility with your placement depending on your layout.

Before assembling all rows you may need to attach a couple of blocks together so they fit on the side of the pinwheels. Watch the quilt diagram for indications where the two blocks being attached need to be sewn together first before they are added to the row.

Assemble into rows and then assemble the rows together to make the quilt top.

As you can see in the upper left corner of the quilt diagram on the right, in order to fit the floral squares to my pinwheel block I need to so SEW the two squares together into a rectangle. That sewn rectangle should then be the perfect size to be added to the side of the pinwheel block. Having those extra pieces as squares instead of rectangles can offer you more flexibility when choosing your placement in the quilt top.

Step 6: Adding the Borders

I give tips in the beginning of the book about adding borders to your quilts. You may choose to change the size of this quilt so I will not give instructions on the number of strips to use.

The borders on the sample of this quilt are made from 6½-inch strips. Measure the sides of your quilt and cut the strips according to length. After attaching the strips to the sides of the quilt, re-measure the quilt for the border strips on the top and bottom of the quilt top.

Join us on the Web

f Cabin in the Wood Quilters

Cabin Quilters

Cabin Quilters

W Cabin in the Woods Quilters

If you enjoyed this book please check out one of the other titles available from Cabin In The Woods Quilters.

All Scrapped Out!
A guide to making a masterpiece from
your unruly collection of scraps.
© March 2011

Still All Scrapped Out!
More ideas for taming
your unruly collection of scraps.
© March 2012

Civil War Sampler
Block of the Month
© January 2009

What A Load of Scraps!
More possibilities for taming
your unruly scraps
© June 2014

Check the website for new releases.
www.cabininthewoodsquilters.com

ABOUT THE AUTHOR

Penni Domikis is the owner of Cabin in the Woods Quilters, a quilt pattern design company established in 2003. A self-proclaimed Jill-of-all-trades, Penni was introduced to quilting by a family friend and combined her love of this new hobby, along with her passions for photography and graphic design, into a thriving pattern design business. As an award-winning quilter, Penni has developed a reputation for breaking down quilt designs into manageable pieces for quilters of all skill levels, following her company's motto, "Make it simple ... but make it with style!" She loves the creativity of coming up with new designs and delights in all aspects of the pattern process, from the cutting, to the stitching, to the print layout for production. She loves meeting quilters all over the country at classes, workshops and quilt shows and enjoys seeing her designs stitched and recreated by other quilters. In addtion to designing patterns and a line of laser cut templates for Cabin in the Woods Quilters, Penni also designs quilts and projects and technically edits for fabric companies, and is the managing partner in an Engineering Consulting firm.

Penni houses her office and design studio in the log cabin lovingly reconstructed by her husband after its catastrophic loss to fire in 1999. Penni's home and wooded surroundings lend more than a name to Cabin In The Woods Quilters. The beauty of the surrounding nature provide her with continual inspiration while allowing the freedom and flexibility to spend more time being a mom. Penni resides in Fredericksburg, Virginia and shares her home with her husband, three sons and three dogs.

The author at work at the cabin in the woods.